Pelican Pete's
BACKYARD ADVENTURES
Nature Discoveries and Outdoor Fun

Frances Keiser

Illustrated by Hugh Keiser

Have Fun Outdoors!

St. Augustin
1/9/16

Sagaponack Books   St. Augustine, Florida

Sagaponack Books is a member of the Green Press Initiative.

Second Printing November 2015

ISBN: 978-0-9668845-7-9

Library of Congress Control Number: 2009906729

Keiser, Frances.
    Pelican Pete's backyard adventures : nature discoveries and outdoor fun / Frances Keiser ; illustrated by Hugh Keiser.--1st ed.
        72 p. 22 cm. Set 1, Volume 1. (Pelican Pete's Backyard Adventures Set 1, v. 1)
    Includes index.
    Summary: A collection of nature facts about plants, animals, and environmental sciences. Each topic includes related outdoor activities, physical games, rhyming verse, and journal pages.
    ISBN: 978-0-9668845-7-9
    1. Nature--Juvenile literature. 2. Poetry--Juvenile literature. 3. Nature study--Juvenile literature. 4. Nature study--Activity programs--Juvenile literature. 5. Nature--Miscellanea--Juvenile literature. 6. Outdoor recreation for children--Juvenile literature. I. Keiser, Hugh, ill. II. Title. III. Title: Backyard adventures. IV. Title: Pelican Pete.

QH48. K458 2009   [508]   2009906729

www.SagaponackBooks.com

Thanks to:

Kathy Shea, Sue Sellers, Beth Mansbridge, and Dena Meyerhoff
for their support and professional services.

And to the following experts for their accuracy checks:

Misty Alderman	Environmental Education Specialist, Office of Environmental Education, Florida DEP
Gen Anderson	Bird and Mammal Curator, St. Augustine Alligator Farm Zoological Park
Dennis Auth	Biologist
Gian Basili	Ornithologist, Audubon of Florida
Ric Bessin	Entomologist, University of Kentucky
Ken Ceglady	Botanist, Environmental Resources Solutions
Keith Fuller	Horticulturist, University of Florida
Beth Geils	Science Educator
Bill Hilton, Jr.	Educator/Naturalist, Executive Director, Hilton Pond Center for Piedmont Natural History
Kevin T. Karlson	Ornithologist, wildlife photojournalist, author
David Kledzik	Herpetologist, Reptile Curator, St. Augustine Alligator Farm Zoological Park
Martin B. Main, Ph.D.	Professor, Wildlife Ecology and Conservation, University of Florida
Dena Meyerhoff	Science and Reading Educator, Exceptional Student Education Specialist
Preston Robertson	Vice President for Conservation, Florida Wildlife Federation
Al Sandrik	Meteorologist, Senior Forecaster, NOAA
John Sivinski, Ph.D.	Entomologist, Research Leader, USDA Agricultural Research Service
Jen Stabile	Herpetologist, Florida Central Zoo
Bob Wattendorf	Freshwater Fisheries Management, Florida Wildlife Conservation Commission
Wm. David Webster, Ph.D.	Professor and Curator of Mammals, University of North Carolina at Wilmington
Patrick Welsh, Ph.D.	Executive Director, Advanced Weather Information Systems Lab, University of North Florida
David Wiles, Ph.D.	Education Professor

The Adventures of Pelican Pete
Rhyming picture book series
A Bird Is Born
Preening for Flight
First Discoveries
Annie the River Otter
Un Ave Nace (*A Bird Is Born*, in Spanish)

For all those who wonder what to do when told to get outdoors ...

"*If we want children to flourish, we
need to give them time to connect
with nature and love the Earth
before we ask them to save it.*"
—David Sobel

Contents

Introduction

Pelican Pete's Backyard Adventures is a book created to help readers, big and small, connect with nature. Filled with interesting facts and no-materials-needed activities, it offers endless possibilities for anyone wondering what to do when told to "Get outdoors!"

Use it as a guide for exploring plants and animals found in your yard or neighborhood, and as a nature journal for you to record new discoveries and to draw illustrations of your observations. You can even download extra journal pages for free at PelicanPete.com, a website where you can learn more about backyard adventures and connecting with nature.

Getting outdoors is a natural way to stay fit, make new friends (wild ones too!), and learn about the environment. So go ahead, get outdoors and explore nature—you'll have fun!

There's so much to learn, discover, and see,
So come on along and explore with me!

Performing Peepers

In southern states, spring peepers peep during the winter! Spring peepers (*Pseudacris crucifer*) are a species of chorus frogs—tiny tree frogs usually heard but not seen. Their loud, clear peeps are made by inflating a large vocal sac and passing air through it. From a distance, the continuous peeping of many frogs in one area sounds like jingling sleigh bells.

Male peepers are the only performers in this annual musical. During breeding season, on warm, rainy nights you may hear them chanting their love song at the water's edge. Each female peeper responds by swimming to the male whose song she favors.

Listen for the calls of frogs, birds, and insects in your yard or neighborhood. Can you hear a pattern in their song? Are they calling to others of their species? How do you know? Can you see the animals and identify them? Imitate the sound. Does an animal answer your call?

Play Performing Peepers! Create your own unique frog-like sounds. Vocalize to one another like the animals do. Can you identify which friend is calling without seeing them? How fast can you hop from one performer to the next?

Performing peepers sing their tune
Under the light of a winter moon,
Charming the ladies all night long
In a musical filled with song!

Animals I've heard in my yard and neighborhood:

Make a list, write a story, or create a poem.

Drawings of animals in my yard and neighborhood:

Snow Symmetry

Most snow crystals have six sides. The crystals form around dust particles carried high into the clouds by the wind. When the temperature is very cold, water vapor clinging to the particles changes to ice crystals. The crystals grow to build symmetrical six-sided (hexagonal) structures.

The four basic crystal shapes are lacy flat disks, prism-like columns, intricate six-pointed stars, and needle-like tubes. All but the tubes are six-sided.

As the snow crystals fall to earth, they join together with other crystals to create snowflakes that land on trees, bushes, the ground, and you—fun!

GET OUTDOORS!

Explore your yard or neighborhood for nature's sixes. Can you find insects with six legs? Flowers with six petals? Spiders with six eyes? Leaves with six lobes? Make a list.

Make clouds! Breathe into cold air and watch water vapor form clouds. Try it against a smooth surface and see how long it takes to evaporate.

Play Six Sticks! Draw two circles on the ground a distance apart. One is a cloud and the other is Earth. Gather six sticks to use as snow crystals and place them in the cloud. How quickly can you race the sticks to Earth—one at a time?

Clouds aloft in a winter sky
Weave coats of crystals from on high,
Made with stars and glittering lace
To cover Earth in a soft embrace.

Nature's sixes I've found in my yard and neighborhood:

Make a list, write a story, or create a poem.

Drawings of nature's sixes in my yard and neighborhood:

Bulb Blankets

Many plants put themselves in storage for the winter. Tulips, lilies, daffodils, and onions are some that create bulbs. The bulb stores a compressed stem, modified leaves called scales, and energy to grow a new plant.

An adaptation requires the bulb to spend a certain amount of time chilled. This prevents new sprouts from beginning to grow during unseasonably warm days. The plant might freeze and die if tender young shoots are exposed too soon.

A bulb protects the stored plant parts like a snug underground blanket through long, cold winters, and keeps them safe.

Ask for permission to dig in a small area. Can you find plant bulbs? Do you see other types of underground storage systems such as tubers or roots? Look for different ways plants store energy to get them through the winter. Look for seeds, nuts, pinecones, and acorns. Note what you find.

Make a Guessing Garden! Gather and plant some of the seeds you found. Circle the area with stones. When warm weather returns, guess what each sprout will become!

Play Springing Sprout! Squat close to the ground like a sprout. How many times you can spring up and down without stopping?

Bulbs keep us safe through winter's breeze
And blanket us so we don't freeze.
When we emerge from underground,
We'll show a lovely flower crown!

Nature's storage systems I've found:

Make a list, write a story, or create a poem.

Drawings of nature's storage systems I've seen:

Excavation Experts

DID YOU KNOW?

Woodchucks (*Marmota monax*) are excavation experts. Digging with strong front legs and pushing aside rocks with their head, they create burrows up to 66 feet long and six feet deep. The den consists of a long tunnel with small toilet chambers to the sides, several escape routes, and a large hibernation and nesting chamber lined with dry grass and leaves at the farthest end.

The burrows and abandoned dens provide shelter for many animals who lack the woodchuck's skillful excavation techniques. In a single day this mammal, also known as a groundhog, removes an average of 716 pounds of dirt!

GET OUTDOORS!

Look closely at the ground in your yard or neighborhood. Can you spot tiny or large openings to burrows? Do you see insects or other animals digging? Are they hiding food? Hunting? Building a home? How do you know?

Be an excavator! Ask permission to dig a small tunnel. Make an exit on each end, and watch to see who moves in.

Play Excavation Expert! Gather some friends and have a race. Which excavation team can push their pile of dirt to the finish line first, using only their hands or a stick?

Digging, digging all day long,
Keeps my body big and strong.
When they put me to the test,
I can tunnel with the best!

Burrows I found, and the animals I've seen there:

Make a list, write a story, or create a poem.

Drawings of animals and their burrows:

Chiseled Choppers

A rat's teeth are always growing. Eastern woodrats (*Neotoma floridana*) use their teeth to cut stems and branches for building nests and to open seeds and nuts for food.

These cute little critters belong to the rodent family. The word *rodent* comes from Latin root words meaning *gnaw* and *tooth*.

All rodents have two front teeth on top and two on the bottom called incisors that grow throughout their lives. These animals must gnaw frequently to prevent their teeth from growing too long. Hard enamel on the front of their incisors and a soft surface on the back keep the teeth sharp as a chisel.

GET OUTDOORS!

Look closely at tree trunks in your yard or neighborhood. Can you find signs of animals gnawing on the bark? Do you see seeds, nuts, and acorns with teeth marks? Leaves with bites taken out of them? What animals do you think have been nibbling? How do you know? Note what you observe.

Make a woodrat! Draw the outline of a cute woodrat in the dirt. Use grass for fur, pebbles or seeds for teeth, and give him a stick to chisel his choppers.

Play Rodent Rodeo! At the signal, quickly round up sticks, acorns, and other items a woodrat might like to gnaw on. Who can gather the most items in three minutes?

Gnawing bark, branch, and limb,
Keeps our teeth short and trim.
Marks on wood show it clear.
See the signs? We've been here!

27

Animals I found nibbling or gnawing:

Make a list, write a story, or create a poem.

Drawings of the animals and teeth marks I've seen:

Sweetheart Serenade

Male mourning doves (*Zenaida macroura*) serenade a mournful song that gives the species its name. The song is performed at the start of the breeding season as the male takes center stage on a carefully selected cooing perch.

If a female takes notice, her suitor begins an aerial display by rising high in the air with noisy wing flaps. He then extends his wings and does a spiraling glide back to the perch. His performance continues on the ground as he bobs his head and struts about with fluffed feathers and puffed breast.

If the female accepts him, they form a strong bond, build a nest, and raise three or more broods together that season.

Listen to the songs of the birds in your yard and neighborhood. Are they singing to attract a mate? How do you know? Can you hear mourning doves cooing? Do you see birds performing courtship displays? Building nests? Note what you hear and observe.

Build *your* nest! Gather sticks and dry grass and weave them together on a low branch. Test your nest by putting three small egg-size rocks in it. Will it hold the rocks?

Play Dancing Dove! Choose someone to be Dove and follow his lead as he or she swoops, glides, flaps, and struts about.

I'll serenade with a mournful song,
Puff up my feathers and strut along;
I'll dive from high in the sky above—
Make you my sweetheart and win your love.

Birds I've heard singing in my yard and neighborhood:

Make a list, write a story, or create a poem.

Drawings of birds and nests I've seen:

Gall Guests

Leaf galls are swellings of plant tissue that can look like balls, blisters, pointed hats, or fuzzy hats. They are produced by the plant in response to an irritation. The most common source are insects that embed themselves into the plant's flesh.

Some types of wasps and gnats find a gall the perfect place to spend the winter. The plants do all the work to build a cushy, warm room for each of their insect guests. The host plant even fills the space with food the insects like to eat.

Throughout the winter, insects in the plant galls are protected from cold, hunger, and most predators. When spring arrives they depart their winter home, leaving the host plant unharmed.

Look in your yard and neighborhood for leaf galls. Can you find different-shaped galls? What do they look like? Do you see galls on other parts of the plants, such as twigs or stems? Which trees or plants are producing them? Do you think an insect is inside? How do you know?

Play Gall Gathering! Divide players into two teams, plants and insects. Each plant holds two acorn "galls." At the signal, insects chase plants. When a plant is tagged by an insect, the plant gives the insect a gall. Which insect can gather the most galls? Change sides and play again.

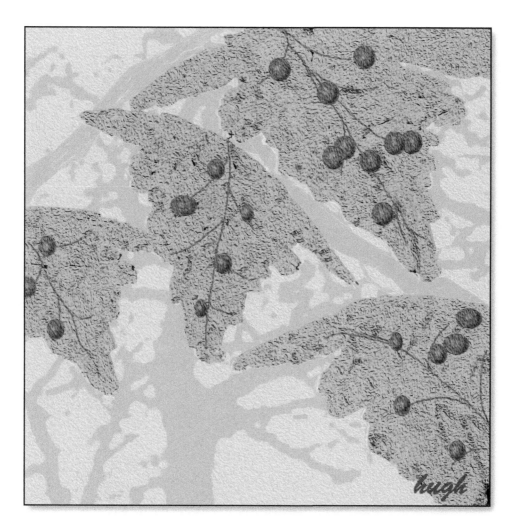

Bumps and lumps and blisters, too;
The dotted leaves are hiding you.
Snuggle up in your cozy rooms,
Emerge when the springtime blooms!

 Trees and plants I've found with galls:

Make a list, write a story, or create a poem.

Drawings of galls and insects I've seen:

Sunning Snakes

DID YOU KNOW?

Eastern indigo snakes (*Drymarchon couperi*) like to spend cold winter nights snuggled in gopher tortoise burrows. Like all reptiles, they do not have the ability to regulate their body temperature as we do. When the air is below 50 degrees, they seek warmth underground.

As the temperature rises, they emerge and bask in the sun to warm themselves. Iridescent blue-black scales on their long, thick bodies help draw in heat. If they begin to get too warm, they must retreat to the shade so they won't become overheated.

GET OUTDOORS!

Look in your yard and neighborhood for reptiles sunning themselves to get warm. Can you see lizards or turtles? Frogs or butterflies? Do *you* feel warmer in the sun? Do you feel even warmer in the sun if you're wearing dark-colored clothes? Place a black stone and a white stone in the sun. Which stone gets warmer?

Make a Sunning Salon! Find a dark, flat rock and place it in a sunny spot. Watch to see who comes to your sunning salon.

Play Rockin' Rock! Gather some friends and pass a rock up and down a snaking line while dancing with snake-like movements and singing a favorite song. The player holding the rock when the song ends gets to choose the next song.

Indigo snake in the shimmering sun,
Stretching his body and having some fun
Soaking up sun rays in the warm daylight—
Sharing a burrow on a chilly night!

Reptiles I've seen warming themselves in the sun:

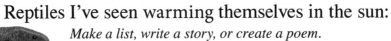

Make a list, write a story, or create a poem.

Drawings of reptiles sunning:

Seasonal Sun

The Earth tilts. Imagine a pole running through the center of our planet, with one end protruding at the North Pole and the other end at the South Pole. This is the axis on which Earth spins, and it tilts at a 23° angle.

As the Earth spins, this tilt causes the length of daylight to change each day. It also creates our seasons. When the Northern Hemisphere leans toward the sun, the Southern Hemisphere is in more shade. This makes it summer in countries north of the equator and winter for those south of the equator.

From your yard, notice where the sun rises and sets, but do not look directly at it. Does the location change each day? At noon, is the sun directly overhead, or is it a little to the north or the south? How do you know?

Make a sundial! Stick a twig in the ground and draw a circle around it. At noon, tilt the stick slightly toward its shadow (to adjust for Earth's 23° tilt). Mark the point where the shadow crosses the circle as 12. Notch and number the circle 11 more times, like a clock, at equal distances. In which direction does the shadow travel around your sundial?

Play Radiant Rays! Pretend you are the sun and your arms and legs are sun rays. Stretch, spin, twirl, and do cartwheels!

Every day a bright sun sets sail
Across the sky like a large whale
Breaching Earth in a mighty leap,
Then diving back into the deep.

Where I see the sun rise and set:
Make a list, write a story, or create a poem.

Drawings of colorful sunrises and sunsets:

Lucky Leaves

White clover (*Trifolium repens*) is a lucky plant for wildlife. Small mammals such as cottontail rabbits enjoy nibbling on the foliage and seedpods. Larks, pheasants, and other birds peck at the leaves or seeds. Clouded sulphurs are one of the species of butterflies that prefer white clover as their host plant. Deer and other grazers enjoy clover, as do farm animals, in their fodder.

Many insects feed on the flower's nectar—especially bees who collect the sugary fluid and turn it into clover honey. Mm-mm … clover is lucky for us, too!

Look for clover in your yard or neighborhood. Find the three leaflets that make up each leaf. Can you find a four-leaf clover? Is it common? How do you know?

Notice the many different shapes of plant leaves. Can you find ones that are round? Oval? Long? Narrow? Shaped like the palm of your hand? A heart? Note what you observe.

Play Plant Puzzle! Players each collect a fallen leaf from several different plants. Without the others seeing your leaves, take turns describing one. Be very detailed and see who can identify which plant it came from. When finished, spread your leaves on the ground and hop from one to the next!

Clover's a plant filled with luck
For doe, fawn, and grazing buck;
For birds, bunnies, and bees, too—
Sweet honey for me and you!

Leaf shapes I've found in my yard and neighborhood:

Make a list, write a story, or create a poem.

Drawings of leaves I've seen:

Sound Sensors

Rabbits use their ears for keeping safe and staying cool! Eastern cottontails (*Sylvilagus floridanus*) have long ears and a keen sense of hearing. Each ear is able to move independently of the other to help them hear sounds from many directions. When alerted to danger, cottontails dash into the underbrush, lower their ears over their backs, and make it difficult for predators to spot them.

On hot days, a cottontail's long ears serve an additional purpose. The large surface draws heat from their bodies and helps to keep them cool!

Sit in a quiet spot in your yard or neighborhood and listen for the sounds of animals. Can you hear a sound better if your ears are turned toward it? If your hands are cupped behind your ears? Do you hear singing? Scratching? Chattering? Chirping? Guess what creatures are making the sounds. Were you right? How do you know?

Play Storyteller Sprint! Choose a home base. Players stand in line together 20 paces away. The first storyteller makes up and tells one sentence to begin a story, then sprints to home base and back. Each storyteller repeats the story, adds a new sentence, and sprints to base. The last player ends the story. Play again.

Hear the sounds around you, of nature's call and song,
Sung by birds in lofty trees with tunes both brief and long.
Hear the scrapes and shuffles of beaks, snouts, and claws,
Digging, climbing, darting, on wings or padded paws.

Animal sounds I've heard in my yard and neighborhood:

Make a list, write a story, or create a poem.

Drawings of the animals I've heard:

Fantastic Flyers

Ruby-throated hummingbirds (*Archilochus colubris*) are fantastic flyers. Each spring these tiny birds travel 1,000 miles or more from Mexico or Central America to breed and nest in eastern North America. High energy requires them to consume at least their body weight daily to meet their needs. Their migration route is timed to the blooming of tubular-shaped flowers in bright, showy colors such as red, yellow, and orange.

Darting among the blossoms, hummingbirds are able to hover in place, fly frontward, backward, and even upside down. The humming sound is made by their wings, which move amazingly fast—up to 200 beats per second!

GET OUTDOORS!

Look in your yard and neighborhood for tubular-shaped flowers. Can you spot hummingbirds among them? Butterflies or other insects? Which flowers attract the most birds and insects? Is one plant their favorite? How do you know? Note the plants and the animals the plants attract.

Play Fantastic Flyer! See how many times each player can flap their arms like wings while someone counts slowly to ten. Who is the fastest? Now, dash quickly between bushes and trees like hummingbirds darting from flower to flower.

I dash and dart and hover too,
I'm busy finding nectar dew
On bush or vine with flowered coat,
To sip into my ruby throat!

Flowers I've seen that attract birds and insects:
Make a list, write a story, or create a poem.

Drawings of flowers, birds, and insects I've found:

Exceptional Eyes

The eyes of a praying mantis are unusual. These graceful creatures have stereoscopic vision, a feature normally found only in vertebrates. Seeing one object with two eyes at the same time enables them to accurately judge distance. With a flexible neck that allows them to move their head in any direction, their two large compound eyes can follow every movement.

Mantids (Family *Mantidae*) hold their front legs in a prayer-like position and sit motionless or rock gently to resemble a leaf—they watch and wait. When prey approaches and reaches the correct distance, the mantis strikes with lightning speed and captures its target faster than *your* eyes can see!

GET OUTDOORS!

Look at the eyes of the animals in your yard or neighborhood. Can you find spiders with eight eyes? Insects with five eyes? Animals with no eyes? Do their eyes follow your movements? Can they see you if you stand motionless? How do you know?

Play Critter Capture! Choose one player to be Mantis. Remaining players are critters. Draw a circle for Mantis to stand in. Mantis remains motionless in the circle while critters approach. How close can critters get to Mantis before Mantis strikes and captures them with a touch? Take turns being Mantis.

Big round eyes are watching you;
Hands in prayer are ready to
Strike out quicker than a flash,
And capture lunch—bug-bite hash!

The shape, size, and number of eyes on animals I've seen:

Make a list, write a story, or create a poem.

Drawings of animals and their eyes:

Common Core Standards

Book As a Whole	
RI.K.6	Name the author and the illustrator and define the role of each.
RI.1.6	Distinguish between information given by illustrations vs. text.
RI.2.6	Main purpose of text.

Did You Know?	

Reading Informational Text Standard

RI.K-5.1	On grade level: Ask questions, answer questions using details from the text.
RI.K-5.2	On grade level: Determine main idea and supporting details / summarize text.
RI.K-5.3	On grade level: Describe and explain connections and relationships between concepts, events, and ideas, based on information from the text.
RI.K-5.4	On grade level: Vocabulary (cross-reference with science standards for domain-specific vocabulary).
RI.4-5.5	On grade level: Describe structure of ideas and concepts / compare with the poem.
RI.K-4.7	On grade level: Relationships between illustrations and text.
RI.K-5.8	On grade level: Explain supporting details and reasons.

Language Standards

L.K-5.4	On grade level: Determine and clarify the meaning of unknown words and phrases using grade-level specifics.
L.K-5.5	On grade level: Demonstrate understanding of word relationships, nuances, and figurative language using grade-level specifics.

Get Outdoors!	

Speaking and Listening Standards

SL.K-5.1	On grade level: Engage in collaborative discussions using grade-level specifics.
SL.K-3.3	On grade level: Ask and answer questions in order to clarify.

Language Standards

L.K-5.6	On grade level: Use grade-specific vocabulary accurately.

Poem	
Reading Literature Standards	
RL.K-5.4	Grade-level discussion on content of the poem.
RL.K-5.5	Grade-level discussion on structure of the poem.
RL.K-5.7	Grade-level comparison of the poem to the illustration.
RL.2-3.9	Grade-level comparison of the poem to the text.
Journal	
Writing Standards	
W.K-3.8	On grade level: Recall information from experience and text.
W.4-5.9	Draw evidence from text to support reflection.
W.3-5.10	Write routinely for discipline-specific tasks.
Language Standards	
L.K-5.1	On grade level: Demonstrate command of standard English grammar conventions using grade-level specifics.
L.K-5.2	On grade level: Demonstrate command of standard English capitalization, punctuation, and spelling conventions, using grade-level specifics.
L.2-5.3	On grade level: Use knowledge of language and its conventions when writing, using grade-level specifics.

For additional activities, journal pages, and resources, visit PelicanPete.com.

National Educational Standards

Did You Know?		
Subject	*Standard*	*Page*
Science		
Life Science	NS.K-4.3	10, 18, 22, 26, 30, 34, 38, 46, 50, 54, 58
Earth & Space Science	NS.K-4.4	14, 42
Physical Science	NS.K-4.2	14, 38, 54
Get Outdoors!		
Subject	*Standard*	*Page*
Science		
Inquiry	NS.K-4.1	10, 14, 18, 22, 26, 30, 34, 38, 42, 46, 50, 54, 58
Life Science	NS.K-4.3	10, 18, 22, 26, 30, 34, 38, 46, 50, 54, 58
Earth & Space Science	NS.K-4.4	14, 38, 42
Physical Science	NS.K-4.2	14, 54
Math		
Numbers & Operations	NM-NUM.PK-2.1	14
Geometry	NM-GEO.PK-2.4	46
Language Arts		
Communication Skills	NL.Eng.K-12.4	50

Physical Education		
Movement Forms	NPH.K-12.1	10, 14, 18, 22, 30, 34, 42, 46, 54, 58
Responsible Behavior	NPH.K-12.5	14, 22, 26, 30, 34, 38, 58
Music		
Performing Rhythms	NA-M.K-4.2	10
Singing	NA-M.K-4.1	38
Dance		
Demonstrating Movement	NA-D.K-4.1	30, 38, 42, 54
Journal		
Subject	*Standard*	*Page*
Language Arts		
Applying Language Skills	NL-Eng.K-12.12	12, 16, 20, 24, 28, 32, 36, 40, 44, 48, 52, 56, 60
Science		
Inquiry	NS.K-4.1	12, 13, 16, 17, 20, 21, 24, 25, 28, 29, 32, 33, 36, 37, 40, 41, 44, 45, 48, 49, 52, 53, 56, 57, 60, 61
Visual Arts		
Applying Media Techniques	NA-VA.K-4.1	13, 17, 21, 25, 29, 33, 37, 41, 45, 49, 53, 57, 61

For additional activities, journal pages, and resources, visit PelicanPete.com.

Index

About the Publisher

Founded in 1999, Sagaponack Books is an independent publishing company dedicated to connecting children with nature. Their award-winning Adventures of Pelican Pete fiction series and Pelican Pete's Backyard Adventures nonfiction series are reliable sources for environmental education as well as useful tools to inspire outdoor exploration and discovery.

Awards and honors:
> Teacher's Choice Award – Learning Magazine
> Children's Choices – International Reading Association
> Book of the Year for Environmental Education – Izaak Walton League
> Mom's Choice Award – Mom's Choice Awards
> Best Products: Children's Books – iParenting Media
> Best Children's Fiction – Florida Authors and Publishers Association
> Best Florida Title – Florida Authors and Publishers Association
> Accelerated Reader listing – Renaissance Learning
> Reading Counts! listing – Scholastic

Present and past memberships:
> Get Outdoors Florida! Coalition
> Green Press Initiative
> North American Association for Environmental Educators
> Children and Nature Network
> The Children's Book Council
> Association of American Publishers
> International Reading Association
> American Library Association
> Association for Library Service to Children
> The Independent Book Publishers Association
> Florida Authors and Publishers Association

To learn more, visit SagaponackBooks.com.

About the Author & the Illustrator

Hugh and Frances Keiser write and illustrate the Adventures of Pelican Pete book series, and a weekly newspaper column—Pelican Pete's Backyard Adventures: Nature Discoveries and Outdoor Fun—to inspire children to get outdoors, explore, and play. The columns became the basis for the Backyard Adventures book series.

Frances Keiser, is a master naturalist certified by the University of Florida, and has over thirty-five years' experience working in wildlife conservation and early childhood education. Her background, coupled with her love for exploring nature, contributes to her writing.

Hugh Keiser is a professional artist working in a variety of mediums for over forty-five years. His award-winning art is displayed in public and private collections around the world. A love and appreciation for art, nature, and children led Hugh to create his popular book illustrations.

The couple lives in St. Augustine, Florida, in a home surrounded by nature, woods, and wildlife, where they enjoy spending time outdoors with their grandchildren and their inquisitive cat, Tina.

With the help of their award-winning books and columns, and through their programs and speaking engagements, the Keisers contribute to environmental education nationwide. The benefit of their work is helping a generation of children connect with nature and get outdoors!

To learn more, visit PelicanPete.com.